There's writing on the bus,
there's writing in the fridge.
Writing on the TV, and
on Sydney Harbour Bridge.

Draw pictures of other places where you can see writing.

Contents and curriculum links

Fl. = Fluency page WYO = Write Your Own page

Sit comfortably.

Hold your pencil lightly.

Turn your book a little bit.

Concepts of writing

Writing is made up of letters and words.

Letters *e g h o s t w*

Words *dog*  *cat*

Spaces *in the tree*

Letters make different sounds in different words.

Spaces between words make it easier to read the writing.

Purpose of writing

Writing is very useful.

You can

tell stories

describe what you see

label things

send messages

make lists

and have fun
with words and ideas.

Letter formation: Cursive style

Most letters start at the top ...

g h s u

... and have strong down strokes.

j k p w

Many letters have crisp turns.

b d o y

Some letters have entries and exits.

a m r t

This makes it easier to do joined writing later on.

Letter formation: Bodies, heads and tails

All letters have a body. Some letters have heads or tails as well.

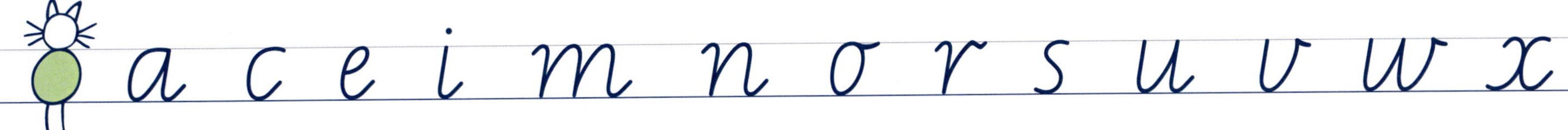

g j p q y z

Reference: Lower case alphabet

a b c d e f g h i

j k l m n o p q r

s t u v w x y z

Write Well!

Reference: Upper case alphabet and numbers

A B C D E F G H I

J K L M N O P Q R

S T U V W X Y Z

0 1 2 3 4 5 6 7 8 9 10

Reference: Starting point and direction for lower case

a b c d e f g h i

j k l m n o p q r

s t u v w x y z

0 1 2 3 4 5 6 7 8 9 10

· starting point ↓ direction · finishing point

Reference: Starting point and direction for upper case

A or A B C D E or E

F or F G H or H I J K

L M N O P Q R S

T or T U V W X Y Z

· starting point ↓ direction · finishing point Alternatives are for left-handers.

Instructions: Anti-clockwise letter formation

Anti-clockwise letters: a c g q d e o f s

a c g q

Start at the top (1 o'clock).
Move anti-clockwise.
Finish letters **a** and **q** with an exit.

d e

Start in the middle.
Move anti-clockwise.
Finish with an exit.

o f s

Start at the top.
Move anti-clockwise.
Letter **o** has an exit.
Letter **f** has a tail and two strokes.

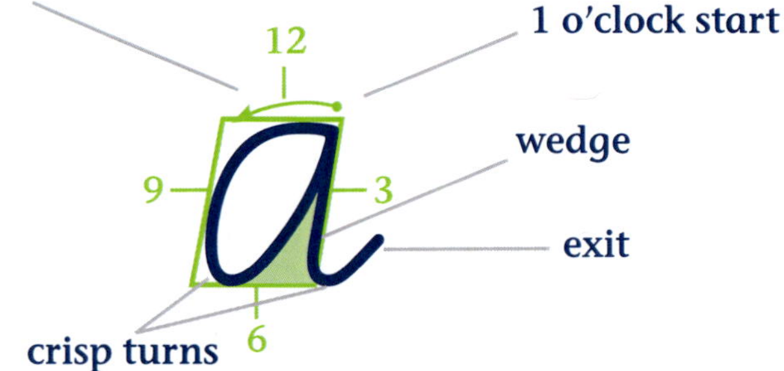

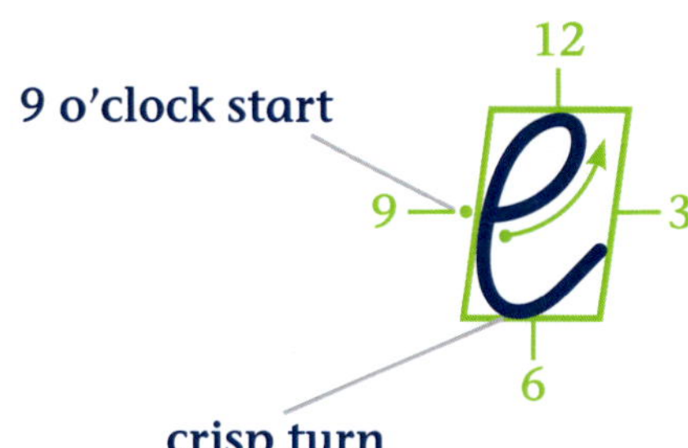

a a a
a a a
apple
c c c
c c c
cut

Anti-clockwise letters d and g

l l l

q q q

q q q

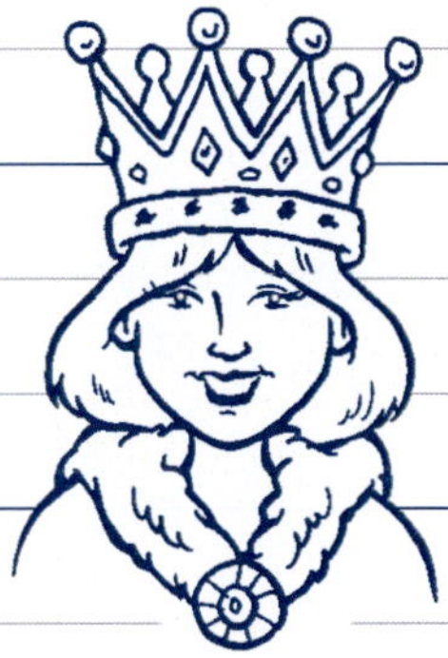

queen

qu qu

qu qu

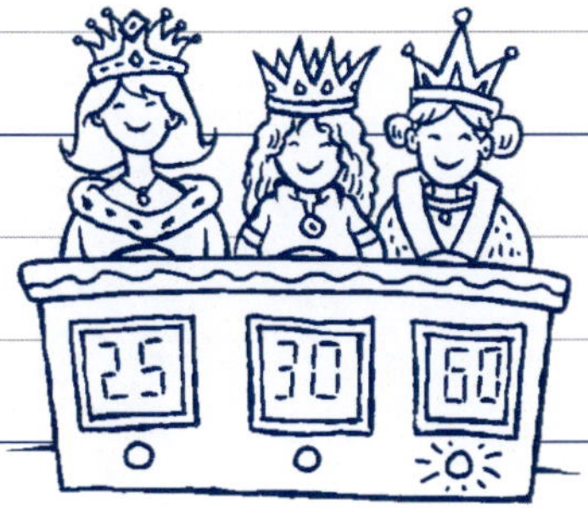

quiz

e e e
oo oo oo
e e e
e e e
emu
o o o
o o o
owl

ff ff ff

f f f

f f f

fish

s s s

s s s

swim

I like movies

I like books

I like the eggs

my dad cooks.

Self-assess

Instructions: Clockwise letter formation

Clockwise letters: m n r x z h k p

m n r

Start with a small entry.
Move down, then clockwise.
Finish with an exit.

x z

Start with a small entry.
Move clockwise.
Letter **x** has two strokes.
Letter **z** has a flattened tail.

h k p

Start at the top.
Move down, then clockwise.
Finish with an exit.

wedge
small rounded entry
crisp turn
exit

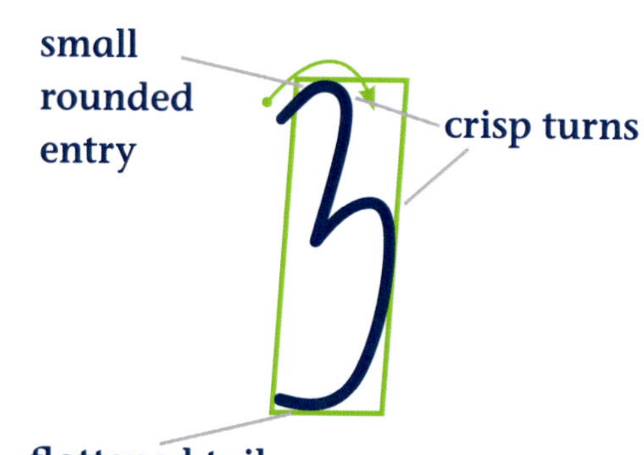

m m m

mouth

m m m

n n n

nose

n n n

r r r

r r r

rope

r r r

r r r

rake

x x x

taxi

x x x

z z z

zebra

z z z

h h h

h h h

house

k k k

k k k

key

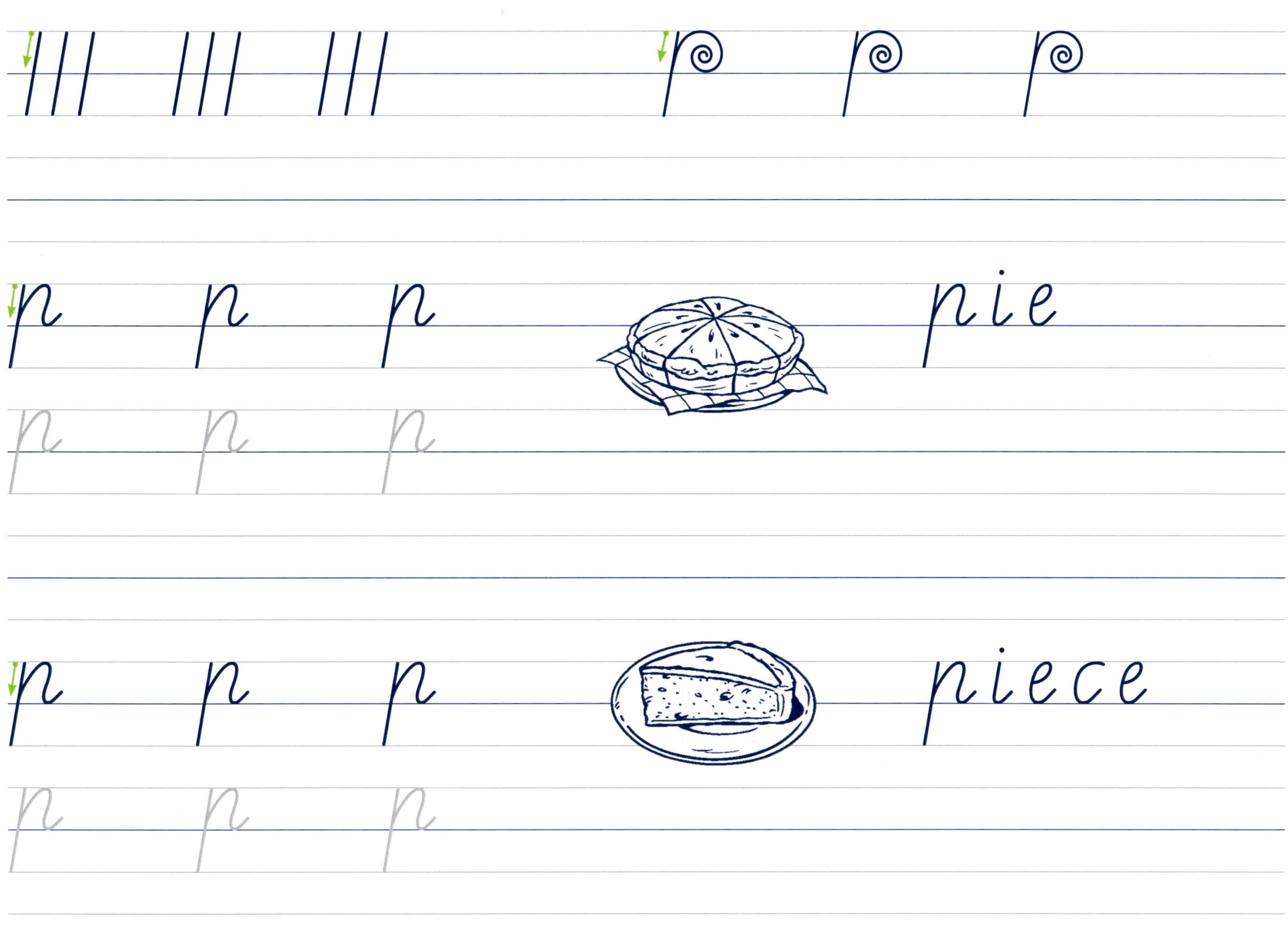
pie
piece

Once upon a time

in a land far away

Sam was

and all day.

peanut butter

cheese and ham

egg and lettuce

strawberry jam

Downward letters: the *i* family **i l t j**

i *l* *t*

Start at the top.
Move ↓ downwards.
Finish with an exit.
Letter **t** has two strokes.

j

Start at the top.
Move ↓ downwards.
Finish with a flattened tail.

First stroke finishes with exit.

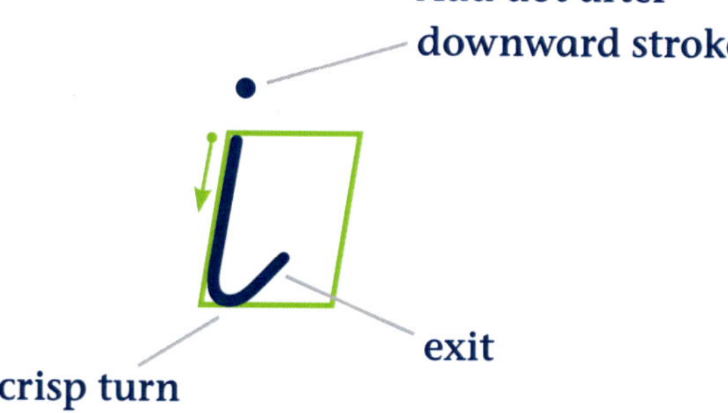

First stroke finishes with exit.

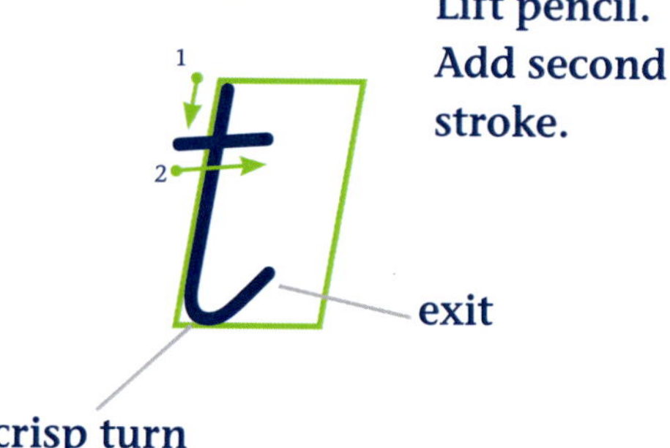

| | | | | | |

| | | | | | |

i i i iron

i i i

l l l ladder

l l l

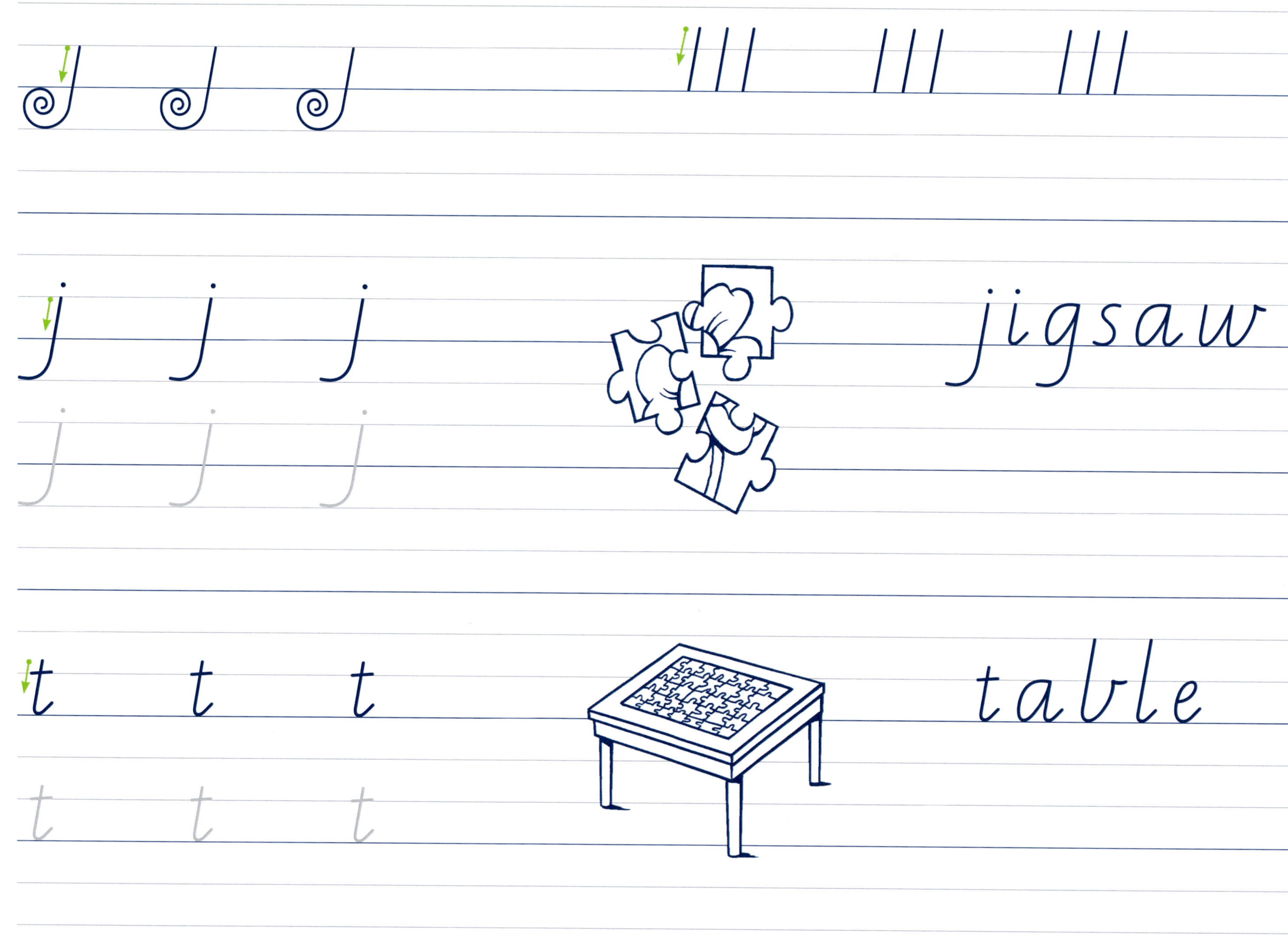
j j j
j j j
jigsaw
t t t
t t t
table

Self-assess

words in words

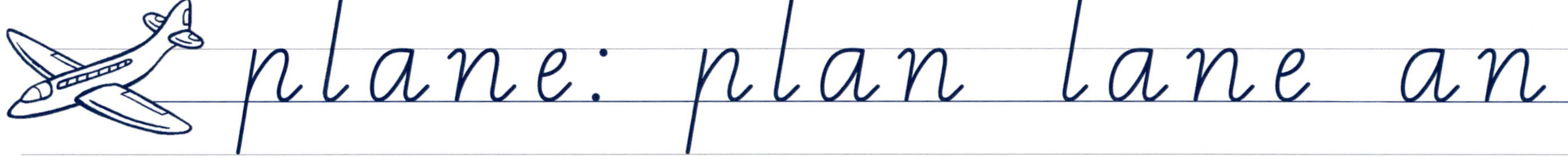

plane: plan lane an

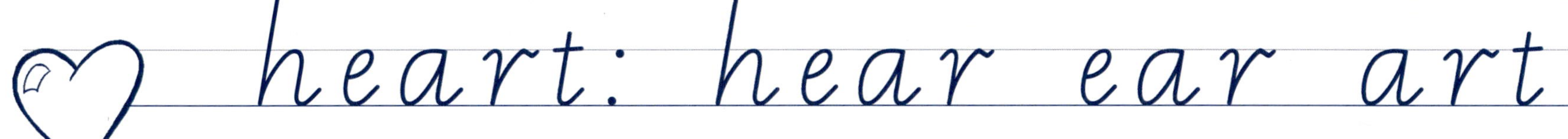

heart: hear ear art

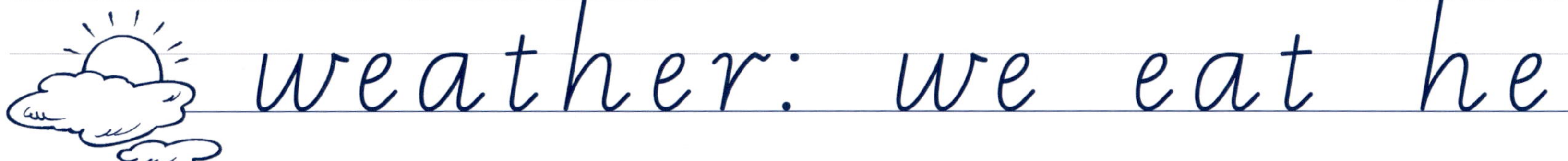

weather: we eat he

What do you like to do best?
Finish these two sentences. Then draw yourself doing something you like.

I like to go

I like to play

Downward letters: the *u* family u v w b y

u v w b

Start at the top.
Move ↓ downwards.
Finish with an exit.

y

Start at the top.
Move ↓ downwards.
Finish with a flattened tail.

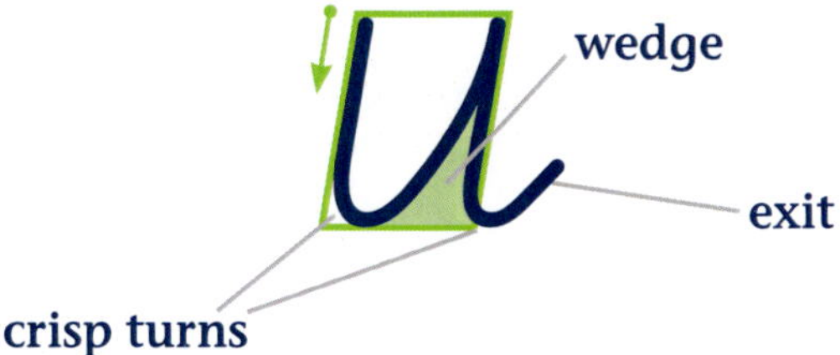

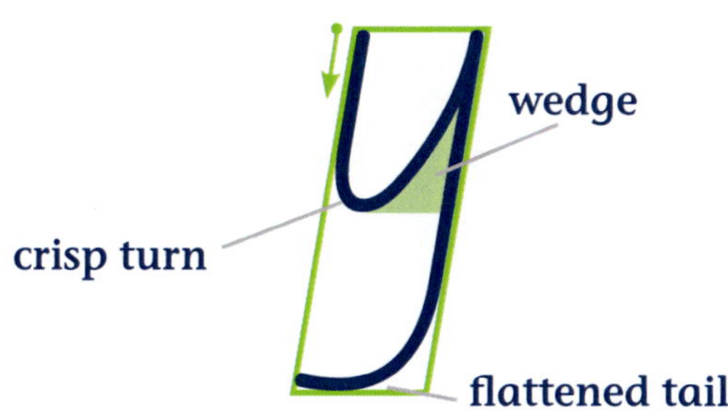

u u u

u u u

u u u

up

y y y

y y y

yawn

Self-assess

ʋ ʋ ʋ ll ll ll

b b b

boat

b b b

b b b

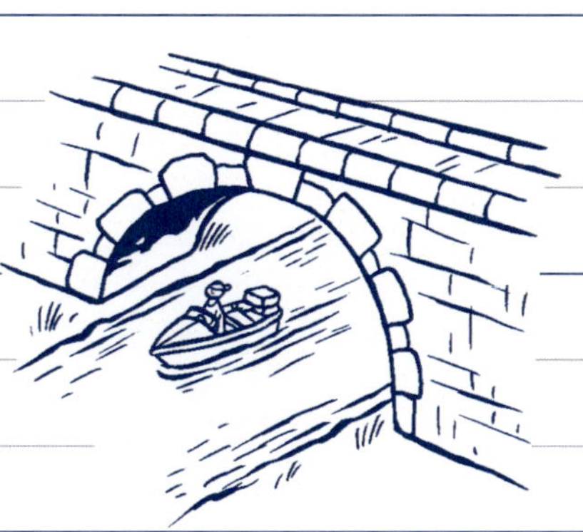

bridge

b b b

v v v v v v

v v v v v v

van

w w w w w w

wash

Why do fish swim
in salt water?

Pepper makes
them sneeze.

BIKE PATH

SHARED PATH

NO BIKES

	Animal	Descriptive words

1 1 1 1 1 1 1 1 1   11 11 11

1 1 1   one

1 1 1

2 2 2   two

2 2 2

3 3 3
3 3 3
three
4 4 4
4 4 4
four

5 5 5 five

5 5 5

6 6 6 six

6 6 6

Self-assess

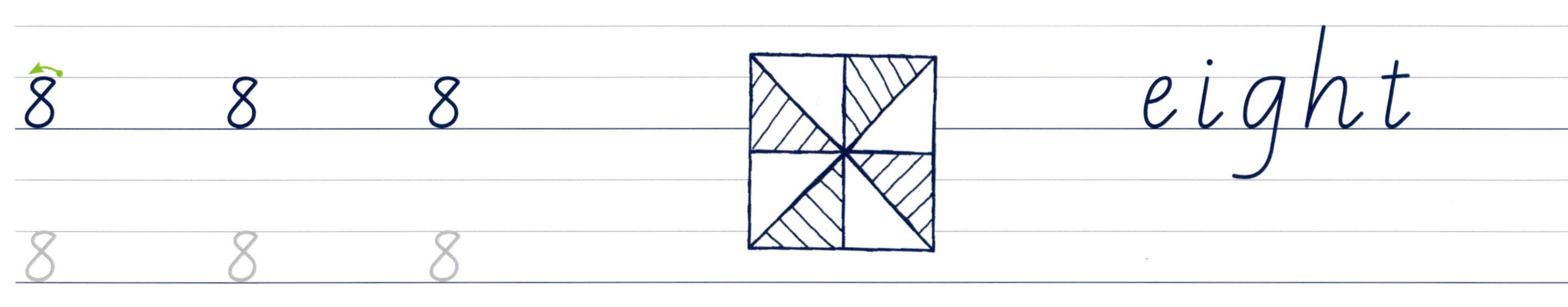

9 9 9 nine

9 9 9

10 10 10 ten

10 10 10

Self-assess

Q: Why was 6 sad?

A: Because 7 8 9.

Echo Mike Lima

two eight four

Thinking about pets

Dogs are clever.

Cats sleep a lot.

Rabbits are fluffy.

Write your own: Story

Self-assess

You can go anywhere you like, using any transport you like.
Where will you go? What will you do there?

My name is

My eyes are

My hair is

I like to write well.